Blind Painting

poems by

JOHN TAMILIO III

For Ann—

Thank you for being part of the team that brought me to Wakefield!

Much love,

WILLIAM L. BAUHAN, PUBLISHERS
DUBLIN, NEW HAMPSHIRE

Library of Congress Cataloging-in Publication Data:
Tamilio, John, 1968–
Blind Painting ; poems / by John Tamilio.
p. cm.
ISBN 0-87233-132-6
I. Title.
PS3620.A68 B58 2001
811'.6—dc21

2001043763
CIP

Some of these poems have appeared in *Artsview*, *Midwest Poetry Review*, *Mobius*, *Prairie Winds*, *Sanskrit*, *Sextant*, *Soundings East*, *South Ash Press*, *WAIL!*, and *Walk Through Paradise*.

William L. Bauhan, Publishers, Inc.
P.O. Box 443
Dublin, NH 03444
Call toll free: 877-832-3738
or visit our website: www.bauhanpublishing.com

Printed in Canada

For Susan,
"the hyacinth girl"

and in memoriam

Thomas D. Robie
28 March 1966 — 28 March 1999

Jason A. DiDonato
28 October 1968 — 5 May 1999

James H. Cunningham, Jr.
9 June 1969 — 10 April 2002

Acknowledgements

There are several people who have inspired the poems in this collection—too many to possibly mention in this brief space. Your influence is deeply appreciated. Your relationships forever cherished.

I thank two people in particular who labored over multiple drafts of this manuscript offering corrections and criticism: my wife, Susan R. Tamilio, and my best friend, Jeffrey M. Gallagher.

I thank my children: Sarah Elizabeth, John IV, and Thomas Jason James. You are angels from God and the inspiration to verse that is yet to break forth.

Finally, I thank the people at William L. Bauhan, Publishers. I thank Bill, for believing in this project ever since he read the original manuscript, and his daughter Sarah, who knows that people do judge books by their covers!

John Tamilio III

I Nausikaa's Shore

II Fragments from the Sea

III Penance

IV Redemption

V Sketches from My Window

I Nausikaa's Shore

Susan: a portrait

I

Her face speaks of Monet
and suspends the moment in undiscovered colors:
a stone for all eternity,
as pure as bone,
as crisp as china.

The essence of flesh:
a powder lighter than talc,
yet more potent than pollen,
etherizes every organ
and makes me forget I am alive.

Housed within is the frame of a figure,
too moist and perfect to be adulterated by song and dance,
by magic and witchcraft.

It knows only light and gives it to all in a smile of childhood,
too fragile to speak,
too honest for innocence.

II

Feline fingers embrace the evening.
Still claws, as soft as oyster shells, grip the darkness.
Light drips from a saturated moon.
Sand flows through her knuckles.

The night drowns in the salt of passion,
a mystique that flows as soft as warm milk
through an open door.

III

I am home now.
The smell of cinnamon calls the boy in from play.
A mother's love is never shattered.

The cave, though vacant,
will soon bear children.

She will cradle them in her arms.
The blanket still holds a piece of the moon.
The night, which cried out to Aphrodite,
calls again and says, "Mother, I am home now."

Of yesterday

Home is where one starts from. As we grow older
The world becomes stranger, the pattern more complicated
Of dead and living.

– T. S. ELIOT, *East Coker*

Of yesterday,
she remembers nothing.

Broken tooth, nail, and bone.
All shards of what was,
dissolved in the abyss of the here and now.

The child is not recollected.
She is a watercolor,
saturated by the here and now and the what must be.

The dog trods damp grass.
He stands by the drain,
but is only remembered in the context of coffee-colored film.

Of yesterday,
she only remembers now.

For Nothing More than You

A Lyric for Susan

Smothering in the heat,
prostrate to Tiresias.

For five days I climb this sweltering mountain
only to find
theses and facts,
debate and obligation.

A Moses to Pharaoh.
Longing for Isaac and Rebekah.

I give you my rib:
wanting nothing more than to lie in the rapture of your bed,
to suffocate in the haven of your neck,
and to die in your arms.

February's Child

To approach the dry abyss of memory
without an eye on tomorrow
is to search only for dust and stone.

I come to this valley and find a maiden:
as fresh as salt water,
as warm as burnt October pine.

We dance in the light of today,
and of what will be,
clasping the hands of children yet born.

She is mother and maiden and wife:
the history of tomorrow,
wrapped in the soft dew of the morning.

Blind Painting

She draws me into her soul with a single breath
where I search for
(and sometimes find)
the answers to the questions
she hides like thorns beneath her ribs.

I come without insurgence:
an impotent conquistador bearing token gifts of gold,
and grails of saving blood,
imploring for admission
into her gentle shelter.

A child greets me at the shoreline
carrying her uncle's secrets of broken fishing boats
between two tight hands,
which she rubs together for warmth
as she anticipates chocolate and fresh bread.

My feeble vessel mounts the ocean's shoulder.
I sail without canvas, blindly painting pictures
of Negro women who sell fish from storefront stalls
as I hurry toward the morning
to meet her for breakfast.

Blue Sunrise

when you look at her what do you see

the flower of your youth that escaped
like the taste of champagne
after falling over frost covered lips

long forgotten words that bounce
off the corners of your memory
rustic poetry, stories by Tolstoy

the final notes of a faded aria
that hang in your warm ears
after the waltz has ended

endless ocean waves that crawl to distant shores
that wait patiently like the spring bud
held tight in the pulp of its bulb

the smile that illuminated your face
the first time you tasted fresh apple pie
the joy of cinnamon dancing on your tongue

the sea-shore-salt-stained crimson eclipse
that lingers over a cloud covered blue sunrise
like the perfume of a lover on your pillow

Susan: a second portrait

I

You:
the child,
a patchwork of yesterdays,

desperately trying
to appease the gods,
to mend splinters of broken glass,
and to solve the mysteries
that surround ancient wars
and find you,
in the morning,
at your kitchen table.

II

"And how," you ask, "did it all come to this?"
The sum of these lives:
spider webs of complex emotions
intertwined in the unnamable.

You long to sit in your father's vegetable garden,
with grass-stained shins
and a long, sandy mane
brushing a button-nosed dirty face,
eating fresh tomatoes with him
as you watch the cool juice
bleed down your arm.

III

Old tides wash old bones
upon your shore:
relics from ancient ships,
forgotten mysteries.

Old bone to new soil.
Old clay to new stone.

On the threshold of tomorrow
you stand barefoot on the sand
with your face to the sea:
the wind wraps your dress around your legs
and runs its fingers through your hair,
your arms open wide
ready to embrace the sun.

Midnight

Again, for Susan

I search for you in dreams:
stumbling through rivers of stone,
across fields of countless crosses.
The horizon laughs in silence.

But in the soft morning light,
which settles gently on the forest canyon,
I find you sleeping like a child
dreaming about loaves of warm bread.

February

The field behind our house
is ripe with apples and corn
during the summer months.

In February the seeds of harvest
are dormant – frozen in the tundra
beneath dusty snowdrifts.

(I think of such things
throughout this month:
the month that you were born.)

And as we drive past foreign fields,
towns, and houses that we will never enter,
I think of our own harvest:

the cherubs that we fashioned
as partners in God's infinite act
of sculpting seas and stars

and I think of the day you were born.
With complete precision and perception,
God decided to touch the earth again.

A Reflection upon Waking

If I dream, I shall dream of thee.
I shall burn thy image into a thousand landscapes.
– J.T.

We drive toward the laggard sunrise – the air
as crisp as the frosted designs that are carved into
winter morning windowpanes – to beat the dawn.

The morning fog loiters breathless in the still air
and crawls across the sleepy orchard, blanketed
with dead leaves and countless drops of tired rain:

a cushion for excited feet – the feet of children
trying to outrun the rising sun by beating sod
into the earth's wet follicles with nimble toes.

This vision, that lies just beyond our fingertips,
tempts me – or rather us both – to gather a harvest
of fresh, golden apples that we can still taste.

II Fragments from the Sea

November

For My Father

Shoulders of proud rock carry me to your shore.
I stand before you: unique in obsolescence.

The plump foam crashes on straight slate sand.
It curls and wedges its seltzer between my pink toes.

On the sunburnt horizon I see my father.
His wooden boat is wise with wear.
The white splintered sides and corners
reveal the strength of its history.

His tired arms pull hearty nets from the sea:
the forgiving water surrenders scaled hosts.
He looks like Jesus.

The cold water now embraces my knees.
My chest is heavy.
This is a load that I can no longer carry alone.

I take another step closer to you.

Cape Ann

For Norman

I had a dream of you the other night,
my grandfather.

You were on the sea, broken,
trolling the ocean's throat in desperation
as your blistered vessel floundered between the waves.

Old photographs tell me what I was too young to remember:
I always imagined that you lost your leg at sea
as I would stare at the bold, gray eyes
within the gray head of gray snapshots,
the eyes of a stranger.

Edgartown: Snapshots of Four Seasons

To look upon that landscape in the early morning, with the sun at your back, is to lose the sense of proportion. Your imagination comes to life, and this, you think, is where Creation was begun.

– N. SCOTT MOMADAY, *The Way to Rainy Mountain*

I - SPRING

The morning thunder claps its hands
and baptizes quiet streets
and rooftops of country shops
with warm rain.

The vacationers,
who passed the evening drinking cold beer
by warm fires in ancient taverns,
now speak of chartered vessels
and Melville.

II - SUMMER

The little boy, having played all afternoon in the sand,
his red, swollen cheeks coated with the day's salt,
hangs lifeless from his mother's arms
and is carried home.

III - AUTUMN

The girls,
who worked all summer
as waitresses and ice cream scoopers,
have saved enough money
to study
at the colleges and universities
of the big cities.

The one with strawberry hair remained behind
and still teaches the rich, ogling old men
how to ride horseback.

IV - Winter

The winter snow sneaks in slow
and steals the summer softly.
Only permanent residents, fishermen, and the faithful
move between the bookstore, wet piers, and empty pews.

Tomorrow will come
and kidnap me from this inn
before breakfast settles.

Sunset: Mousam Lake – Part I

The bass I almost caught:
slicing the glassy surface of the blue-black lake with razor fins,
the taut line straining the bloodied gills
and the blistered jaw.

"Come on," I say, as if to convince him
that surrender is in his best interest.
The fight, however, is his.

The snap of the line causes me to fumble:
a drunkard waltzing for whiskey,
a powerless little man.

Drowning

Field to fjord,
old clay to new stone,
stubborn horses
with gnarled manes,
oak and elm,
branches brushing
the wind's hair
and the rusty grains
of cracked rock.

Blue crab,
clawless crustacean,
surfaces and surrenders,
bubbles of foam
escape shuttered orifice,
host of ancient algae
and brittle barnacle,
old shells to new beach,
season to season.

Outer Banks, North Carolina

Thursday, 26 September 1996

Like Odysseus, filled with lust and vanity,
I fight to break free from the mast
that holds my feet in concrete,
safe from the Sirens' wall.

I am lured by song
and the belief that I am immortal.

Relatives of the amoebae and algae
that carved my brain and ribs
through innumerable hours of friction,
sculpting each crevice like the formation
of some ancient river,
force themselves down my lungs
like the semen of a rapist.

Pulled by my ankles beneath the warm, soapy froth,
my shins scrape and bleed from barnacle blistered shells,
moss-covered rocks, and shards of sand.
I engulf chests of water, as strong and sweet as methanol,
and thirst for a mouthful of air.

The voice in my head tries to coax me
to take just one more breath of the noxious liquid.
It assures me that it will all be quick and painless,
as painless as my birth.

First Cut Fish

These thoughts I bring with me
beneath the ocean waves:

Memories of you,
of lost time,
and lost opportunities,
the lost boy, struggling to breathe.

Images borne down long
forgotten hallways,
hallways forged by fire
and atonement.

The face that rises from the darkness
to meet me is that of Athena
carved in stone older than time itself,
as old as creation—
when God first spoke,
when the sea first cut fish,
and I first saw you.

Martha's Vineyard

Many a green isle needs must be
In the deep wide sea of Misery,
Or the mariner, worn and wan,
Never thus could voyage on–

– PERCY BYSSHE SHELLEY,
Lines Written Among the Euganean Hills

The ocean shell
and the crest of your cliffs
hold you in the cusp of their hands
as gentle as splinters of brittle glass.

You are beauty personified:
the lust of ages wrapped in wet-lipped children,
the faces of ships, and salt water lovers.

The demands of time are obsolete
compared to the serenity in which you lie
like a sore old man in a white wicker rocking-chair.

Your strawberry air is as fresh as December frost,
kissed with the scent of burnt October leaves.

(You ask nothing,
yet in return give everything.)

A garden before the fall.
An eternal haven for hope and desire
blessed by the blood of the cross
and the love of God.

Sunset: Mousam Lake – Part II

(A Prose Reflection upon Ordination)

My father was my first professor of natural theology. When I was eight years old, my parents bought a camp on Mousam Lake in Acton, Maine. To this day I look forward to vacationing there with my own family. Each summer I relive the experience of fishing with my father: a very sacred act. During the moments before the rising of the sun, or just before it would sink into the horizon, we would get into our aluminum boat and go to our favorite fishing spot in the cove around the corner from our campsite. During those moments – when tired rays of sunlight would settle onto the glassy surface of the blue lake, when the soft wind would wrap us with the fragrance of countless pine needles, when the only sound we heard was a chorus of bullfrogs, crickets, and loons – during those moments, my father introduced me to the presence of God. During those moments I saw the face of God in each bird that settled on the pieces of brown driftwood off our bow. During those moments I heard the voice of God in each gust of wind that sent the trees on the shoreline into a dance all their own. During those moments, as I looked across Mousam Lake, I realized that my father had brought me to the place where heaven and earth met – the place where God moved around us and through us. Catching fish became irrelevant.

Water

Again, For My Father

I have always wanted to return to the water:
liquid innocence, uniting creation and procreation.

The naked child fumbles pails that quench the circuits of his skin.

To return to the water requires the true humility of virginity.
The water breeds a darkness imperceptible to human eyes.

The young maiden's blood stains the ocean's froth, but is soon diluted.

I have returned to the sea:
the bond of life, age, and time is complete.

The old man pulls his catch into the boat, and the two are one.

III Penance

Dying – Part I

For Joseph Salvatore

I have searched within my lungs
and the space between thought and pen.

I have torn handfuls of soil from the earth,
flinging them into the air
like a madman searching for old bones.

I have screamed cries of hate and passion
till my chest filled with blood.

(I have killed myself a thousand times.)

I have locked myself into a web of pain
and forgot names and faces I used to remember.

(I have been lying to myself for years.)

I have seen the face of despair looking down at me
from my bedroom ceiling at night.
It laughed and told me I will drown
searching the sea floor for my childhood.

Crucified

Embers of incense
smoldering in a silver bowl
waft through this temple
with the fervor of a toddler
fumbling with new language.

I gaze into your stone-carved eyes
and imagine – as if I were there – that
I would have lifted you from your cross, and
I would have draped you in a white robe, and
I would have kissed the wounds on your hands

or maybe I would have just stared into your eyes:
charred liked tired embers in a silver bowl.

Penance

I am haunted by nightmares
of an aged Hitler
in a kerosene lamp-lit loft
ordering two Jews to flog another,
their switches splintering against a motionless buttocks
between bales of sour hay,

of turnpike truck drivers
miles away from home,

of stripped and skull crushed cattle
lining the highway,

of the drunken father,
marinated in the stubble stench of stale whiskey and tobacco,
stealing his daughter's innocence
from beneath her sky blue dress
on the floor of a crippled barn,
still damp from yesterday's rain.

Holocaust

For Viktor E. Frankl and Sonia Weitz

We can skin the walls of strip-show
or strip the skin from human flesh.
Man's potential for cruelty is limitless.

In Auschwitz and Dachau
we were so close to the truth,
but we chose to drive onward.

I came to this place looking for answers,
but all I heard were the echoes of a harmonica
and your father asking you for one last dance.

Man's search for meaning
has been smothered and bludgeoned by the scream of a woman
who bleeds and burns under a black boot.

Pantomime

The morning sun brings me a new compromise,
like one of the thousand little deals
that I have made with God
over the years:
the dull razor across my arm
or the empty bottle under my bed.

I have walked for miles in these broken shoes,
but have only traveled as far as the darkness
that looks into our bedroom window.

Our dance is one of masked lovers
who have surrendered to silent confessions
made on blistered knees in dusty rooms:
confessions as quiet as the space that grows
between blades of brown grass
or the soot between the cracked kernels
on the paw of a black cat.

Beantown, America

I am Boston, Massachusetts:
the shin-scraped and soot-stained streets
speckled and sprinkled with pushcart vendors,
the vacant eyes of the homeless
scavenging for spare change
and scraps of stale sandwiches,
a steel-string subway serenade
wrapped in the shriek of squealing wheels
and the scent of yesterday's urine.
I am the wobbled cobblestone walkways of Quincy Market
and the cigarette butts that line the Charles.
I am the desperate HIV junkie, Jezebel in her torn fishnets,
and the street-corner preacher trying to save them both.
I am the beer-embalmed frat-boys
stumbling down Landsdowne Street
bragging about last night's fuck,
the dilapidated tenement houses that line route nine
and the faces of the black cherubs
that peer through their windows.
I am a blue-gray Monet hanging in the MFA,
the bleacher bums on Yawkey Way,
and the green banners that hung over the parquet.
I am the laughter, the mumble and the hum
that linger beneath clouds of corridor smoke
moments before the Pops explode.
I am the Mick, the spic, the nigger, wop, and Polack,
the tux-and-fur-lined cocktail parties
that light up over Beacon Street after curtain call.
I am the ten year old Roxbury girl
lying in her graffiti playground after the drive-by
staring at my ceiling of sparkling stars
wondering if God can hear me.

Retreat

For Douglas

Wrapped in the dawdling embers of a dying moon
there is a break in consciousness – like the breath
just before the rock pierces the lake's surface
or the pulse that shoots through the finch's wing,
and like the morning flower that awaits the sleepy bee
or the dust that settles on porches after lemonade,
I recall the time that we built crude forts
and played war in the woods behind our house,
the place where we stamped excited feet
into the banks of a withered river bed,
where we sucked the acrid juice of bruised crab apples,
and scraped our shins on the crumbled foundation
of a house long since consumed
by the thirst of fire.

Hallucination

For David

I remember the time
that my brother filled his lungs with helium
and spoke like an elf at my birthday party.

I was afraid that he would never
get his voice back again.

Wedding Dance

For Debra Lynne

I am beginning to accept death
and to understand your spirituality:
the utter consummation
of darkness and light,
of spring dew and brittle fall leaves.

I can fathom the fall of Troy,
Delphic prophecy,
and the Messianic Age:
ancient women searching for cups of gold
or fresh water to cleanse morning sin.

But in the distance between,
before the two become one,
I wish to have one last dance with you,
my sister.

Dying – Part II

Scaling the mountain's face
(dirt, stone, and moss)
the boy returns to the dawn.

The cracked cornice issues forth
a slim stream of water.
Gargled from the broken surface,
where he stands,
it gathers grains of dirt and sand
and brown blades of grass,
smoldering in the sun,
as it forges new trails
through dry soil.

The boy opens his palms to the sun.
He is at prayer
ready to bleed.

IV Redemption

Redemption
(Part III of "Communion")

And all shall be well and
All manner of things shall be well
When the tongues of flame are in-folded
Into the crowned-knot of fire
And the fire and the rose are one.

– T. S. Eliot, *Little Gidding*

I

The soft sound of a burning rose
and the glow of distant lamplight
beckon me to ancient temples
to search for hidden secrets
in empty graves.

Cloaked in the serene darkness of midnight,
I sing praises to you,
praises long forgotten like old men in distant wars.
I drink wine from old skins and vials of ivory,
hoping for tomorrow and looking for comfort
in unspoken words.
My thoughts contain only fragments of what was.

I turn to the sound of a flute, distant,
heard only in the wings of memory.
The notes trickle and drip from my ears
and fall down my face
to wash away this old sin.

II

I come to you again, the sea.
Your crisp surface: forging, cutting, and forgiving.
Replacing all that was lost in time and memory
with new ashes.

Each pulse a new rhythm, a new descent.
Each rib a new fossil, a new generation.

Here I find only what I have been carrying
to place on the altar of your shore,
hoping, by chance,
for new miracles and new messiahs.

Here I try to learn your secrets
as I search beneath pieces of broken rock
for old bones.

III

The tears of our ancestors and the sounds of our own rage
are no longer heard. The echoes have become too distant.
What was can be forgotten with hope and prayer
as we search between words and breaths for redemption.

Field to fjord,
old clay to new stone.

In communion with history,
all that was,
all that is,
and all that shall be,
the child embraces the eternal dawn.

V Sketches from My Window

Writing Poetry

I love to write poetry when it rains.

Between the steam of chai tea
and the warmth of fresh bread
the words seem to drip from my pen
and form dark pools on my page

as I sketch gray puddles
covered with orange leaves
outside my window.

Smoke

We spent that afternoon,
after the rain,
like content cats
propped on our sill,
entwined,
gazing out the window
with only two cups of tea
between us.
The sun was burning the rain
that had fallen on the hot-top
while we made love
that summer morning.
The rays cut through
columns of loitering haze.
(Everything was ours
and we knew it.)
You asked of my love for you.
"My love," I said,
"is like the sun
that burns the soft rain
off the warm pavement
beneath our window sill."

Infidels

What's a sweetheart like you doin' in a dump like this?

– BOB DYLAN

I fell in love with the way you drank coffee.
You cradled the white cup between both palms with caution:
an innocent child afraid of spilling the warm froth.
Each sip brought a smile to your face.
The rich cream felt so good.

You said something about education,
children,
the beauty of language,
and Spanish conquest.

If I could have fit you into my pocket,
into the corners of my life,
corners reserved only for prayer,
then I would be able to take you out
and I would be able to understand everything you said,
the smile on your face,
and the pleasure of warm coffee.

Untitled

You drifted to me
from out of the darkness
of a thousand doorways:
an apparition – you consumed my flesh
in the stillness of your breath.

Alone, blinded by an eternity of thought,
I recreate you from the ashes of memory –
building you, stone by stone. I cannot escape
nor can I breathe: your scent fills my chest,
your lips upon my neck as we move, like dancers,
into the future: a field frosted green,
illuminated by the morning sun,
immune from the coming harvest.

Now and Then

The telephone rings. "Hello," she says.
"It is so nice to hear your voice
after all these years."

I am so distant from you now
that I no longer feel the pain
or the pulse of the blood
racing through blue veins
at the sound of your voice.

I am learning how to shed my skin
and how to bury it deep
within the cold soil:
my fingers dislodging fragments
of broken skull
and the blood of Abel
calling to God from beneath
his brother's club.

After all these years
I still search for you.

Now and then you enter a dream,
or a breath I take,
but soon disappear
like steam in the cool air.

Sometimes, when I look to the sea,
or scavenge vacant beaches
like seagulls searching for tired crustaceans,
you appear again,
but eventually I am left
with only echoes that fill
a world full of dry bones

after all these years.

Cathy's Song

Memories are often stories
that have been passed down
from generation to generation.

She dangles on the end of the telephone line for hours
in search of something she has lost:
a mother's love or some ancient god.

Her tears drench a brittle letter
that she has memorized.
It was written to a child long ago.

Her pain, now empty, possesses the night
and finds a cavern of rest
in the chest of a husband.

Coffee: A Prose Poem

For Mom

7 o'clock AM.
Mom and Dad arrive home from a two-hour drive.
I stand in their presence dripping wet, wrapped in a towel.

Mom's face is stained red from tears.
It's been that way since we heard the news.
Dad's face hangs an expression of exhaustion, but he always looks that way.

Mom doesn't say much.
She heads straight for the back hall to tend to some leftover ironing.
That's the way she is.
No matter how bad things get, Mom always makes time for her chores.

The sound of my voice pierces through the hiss of the iron.

"How's he doing?"

"Not too good," she replies. The steam rises from her fingers. "He's got this tube the size of my pinky running down his throat forcing him to breathe, and IV tubes all over his body keeping him alive." The tears begin to escape their captivity. "He's never going to make it."

Mom puts the iron down for a moment to wipe her face.
I console her, something I rarely have to do.
Mom usually does that.

Mom's a fighter. She always has been.
Just like Uncle George.
He's even licked leukemia, but I guess the coma has got the best of him this time.

"Auntie Harriet called last night, Mom. She wanted to see how you were."

"I know. She called us in Maine. I have to call Norman to see when he's going back up to see George. I want to go with him." Mom turns towards the stove. "When is the coffee going to be done? I have to go to work."

Two

Double-knuckled limbs
communicate a language
most will never hear.

Forever, We Are

Forever, we are
without a moment's end, stars
cast in destiny.

A Prayer for My Daughter

For Sarah Elizabeth

Before you walk on midnight
as thin as the ocean's skin
and the silk of the moon's halo

remember to turn once – and
as the wind curls your hair
against your feathered brow

say a prayer of thanksgiving
for the grace of morning rays
showered upon you like manna

and the sweet nectar that has
redeemed you from
the silence of ashes.

Lazarus

Un conte de fée pour Jean

Whether dust settles on stone,
or snow on patient fowl feather,
I am unaware.

My tale is story:
an evangelist's tool
to proclaim the kingdom.

My desires, whatever they were,
are as sterile as desert grass
hoisted on a bier

to bring back the sun king,
the hunt of the wren,
thumbprint on steel.

August Drought

For Thomas Jason James

When I was a little boy, I soared above him —
cautious of every footfall, an angel
whispering anonymous poetry,
mimicking the pulse in the sparrow's throat,
beating inviolable wings with my wooden heart
into his stone, implacable ear

the soft anticipation of nothing

wondering if nightfall would shatter the remains
of whatever hopes I managed to salvage
from a day without rain.

Harbinger

"Last of all, as to one untimely born,
he appeared also to me."
— 1 Corinthians 14:8

Epistolary omen,
apocalyptic admonition
steaming under the blood
of crucified martyrs,
intolerant and inerrant
as you rage with your pen,
fervently gouging papyrus,
building history
from the dust of Damascus:
the thorn piercing your side
as it pierced the Christ,
as it pierced Adam.

The vision you gave us —
both Jew and Greek,
slave and free —
sagacity for the evangelists,
or was it the other way around?
The bellow of your call
to complete righteousness
still splits the sky.
The stigmata of your soul
hangs in countless cathedrals
on the lips of stone-carved saints
and the aftertaste of Mass.

Dying — Part III

Channeled Vespers

The hay field is vacant
save a ubiquitous mist
and the sparrow's call
skipping across the river.
The breathless pulse
of dawn's rhythm
deafens virgin soil.

And his eyes, still blue, peer
through the blindness.

Nothing moves.

I stand naked
scooping stars with broken hands
offering water to Gemini
scarred and orphaned.
Nocturnal rusted wreckage
strewn about my wounded feet.

How many deaths have I entered?
And how many men have I loved like this?

And as I stand between thirsty stalks,
absorbed by what lies on the horizon,
I remain vulnerable
to fallen feather
and wounded prey.

Fragments from "The Decad"

I

This endless, solitary trek I make
across this desert of highways
in search of an oasis or a pasture
encumbered by scorching days
and frigid nights:
the rise and fall of mercury,
plasma and history.

My people are a water people:
we are like water spilled on the ground,
which cannot be gathered up – the dust
of the earth – the blood of generations.

And you – you are the mystery,
the apparition that haunts countless dreams
and visions, and, upon waking,
finds the morning much like an old friend
or a distant grandmother
whose sauces still erupt
in the kettles of memory.

But I, however, I remain,
and speak of Solomon speaking of trees
and baptize gods in the desert.

We have the gift and the promise
that the desert shall one day rejoice
and it shall blossom.

III

Holy God,
I am burning.

I come before you
wrapped in the aroma
of candles and darkness.

I come before you on my knees
with my head bent in supplication,
thirsting for divine inspiration
and praying the saint's prayer,
offering my life as a sacrifice
if you will only have me,
I pray.

The grace of God comes burning like the fire
of Babylon's chariots – and it flows
like the waters that once blessed Eden's soil
healing unworthy, blistered souls that thirst

to be saved from the ashes that cover
generations of dry bones that remain
beneath the silent soil and the rocks that
once formed the stalwart walls of Jericho.

Holy God,
I am burning.

I come before you
as a humble servant
beseeching your mercy.

I come before you knowing that
I am not worthy of your grace, nor
am I worthy of the sacred fire
and the healing water
through which you cleanse my bitter spirit
from the stain of Abel's blood.

Here, offering this life,
I pray.

IX

This passion is insurmountable:
like the feathered dance of young lovers
who softly slip through each other's skin
without premonition or caution,

or the moment – the breathless, waking
moment – between sunrise and birdcall.

I will follow her to Jerusalem.
Her people will be my people.
Her God will be my God.

The rustic ruins of some fossil left their mark that remains
as ageless as pieces of moonlight, harbingers for sailors,
and drifts silently on the ocean's back, stirred only by broken,
impotent desire and the last waves that ripple through
the shallow lungs of some dying cetacean.

This is my home now.

I am the last court jester: the one
who danced for courtiers and kings.

I am the last mystic: the one
who forgot the value of prayer.

I am the last fisherman: the one
who never made it home to port.

I am the last criminal: the one
who mocked the crucified Christ.

Pray, let me linger
till my soul flies free,
then cover me with brown leaves
and drop me in the sea.

A Healing

"Your muscles are thirsty," she says,
holding me in the cusp of her palms.

I lay listless in her warm cathedral
where Celtic pipes and hollow voices
lull me across fog-swept Scottish moors,
as I lay dying.

Her hands, as warm as feathers,
the fresh wings of a young sparrow,
reach down the scale of my back.

"Lean back on my hands," she says,
whispering into my left ear.

Her fingers unfold and climb
ridges of ribcage, this sculptress:
healer of bruised bone.

"Your muscles are thirsty," she says.
I mumble something beneath my breath.

Tell me about raindrops – when
the moon was soft and brown,
long ago, before nightfall and birchwood,
tiger lilies and honeycomb.

She whispers, "What?"
and continues her magic.
This conjurer, guiding me
into the depths of my belly.

If I am ever trapped in the depths of Hell
and am surrounded by a thousand furies –
suffering a thousand deaths –
and find myself running
through corridors of countless nightmares,
will you search for me?

She whispers into my left ear,
"You are healed."

Book design by Sarah Bauhan and Iain Bain
Set in Fred Smeijers' FF Quadraat
Printed in Canada